MI6 SPECIAL OPERATIONS
BY ORDER OF THE OFFICE OF THE DIRECTOR

CLASSIFIED: ULTRA / MAGIC [Strictly eyes only to named personnel]; deniable

COPY TO: "C" / Archives / Covert Weapons / Personnel

DESCRIPTION: A covert intelligence-gathering operation targeted at the **SAYLE ENTERPRISES** factory complex in **PORT TALLON**, Cornwall. Map ref. follows: SW821352. Operation is deep-cover, fully deniable.

AGENT(s) ASSIGNED: **IAN RIDER (0223-56)**

MISSION BRIEF:
- Infiltration of Sayle Enterprises security team. Report on Darrius Sayle's activities.
- Fully-backstopped cover story in place — agent is to be employed on Sayle Enterprises security team.
- **RULES OF ENGAGEMENT**: **Any** and **all** necessary force to be employed in the event of mission compromise.
- Full debrief 11 March, Special Operations, HQ.

EQUIPMENT REQUISITION:
- Modified BMW Z4 series
- Yamaha WR450F off-road motorcycle
- Standard CX Intelligence Kit

"I had
a little
trouble ...

SAYLE ENTERPRISES

RI D

but I think I've left it behind me..."

IAN RIDER

Chelsea Courier

Local Man dies in car accident

Ian Rider, of Cheyne Walk, died in a car crash in Cornwall on Wednesday night. Rider, a European Finance Officer with the Royal and General Bank, apparently lost control of his vehicle near Port Tallon. "This was a tragic accident," said a police spokesman. "Our thoughts are with the family and friends." Rider, who was 42, is survived by his nephew.

STORMBREAKER™

BEHIND THE SCENES

Isle of Man Film, UK Film Council
and Entertainment Film Distributors
present a Samuelson Productions
and VIP Medienfonds 4 Production
in association with
Rising Star

**Sarah Bolger   Robbie Coltrane   Stephen Fry
Damian Lewis   Ewan McGregor   Bill Nighy
Sophie Okonedo   Alex Pettyfer   Missi Pyle
Andy Serkis   Alicia Silverstone
Ashley Walters and Mickey Rourke**

Additional Martial Arts Sequences Donnie Yen
Casting Director Sarah Bird
Costume Designer John Bloomfield
Hair & Make-Up Designer Kirstin Chalmers
Associate Producer Jessica Parker
Line Producer Kevan Van Thompson
Editor Andrew MacRitchie
Production Designer Ricky Eyres
Director of Photography Chris Seager, BSC
Executive Producers Hilary Dugdale Nigel Green
Anthony Horowitz Andreas Schmid
Screenplay by Anthony Horowitz based on his novel
Produced by Marc Samuelson Peter Samuelson
Steve Christian Andreas Grosch
Directed by Geoffrey Sax

SAMUELSON PRODUCTIONS    isle of man film    VIP Medienfonds   UK FILM COUNCIL LOTTERY FUNDED

 entertainment film distributors   International Sales by Capitol Films    Alex Rider™ novels published by Walker Books (UK) and Penguin Young Readers Group (USA)    DOLBY IN SELECTED THEATRES   Kodak Motion Picture Film

Contents

The Horowitz INTERVIEW

By EMIL FORTUNE

Anthony Horowitz's phenomenally successful series of books about teen superspy Alex Rider has delighted children all over the world since the first book, *Stormbreaker*, was published in 2000. His career has now taken an exciting new turn, as Alex's first adventure hits the big screen.
I caught up with Anthony to ask him how the movie *Stormbreaker* came about.

■ **So how does this whole book to a movie thing work?**

Well, the author gets a phone call. A producer wants to meet him or her. They get together in a smart restaurant and the producer – often a man with a beard and sunglasses – does this big thing about how much he loves the writer, admires his work and would give anything to buy an option on the book. An option is a sort of down-payment. It's not a lot of money but the producer promises that when the movie is actually made the writer will receive a cheque with lots of zeros and the movie will be a huge hit!

■ **But who actually writes the movie script?**

The producer hires a screenwriter to "adapt" the book. The screenwriter may decide to drop half the action, change the main character, throw out the best jokes, add some new ones and move everything to the moon before he or she is fired. Several more screenwriters will then do the same

Anthony makes his feature film debut!

thing. Meanwhile, the author is sitting at home, waiting for the premiere of his masterpiece, but nine times out of ten, it never comes. The producer gets fed up. The movie goes into what is cheerfully called "development hell" – it never appears!

■ **So how did you avoid this on *Stormbreaker*?**

Four years ago, I was approached by a producer called Marc Samuelson – who did, incidentally, have sunglasses and a beard! He invited me to a fancy restaurant and asked to take out an option not just on *Stormbreaker* but on all of the Alex Rider books. I'd already had other offers but there were two things that really stuck out about Marc. One, he understood what the books were really about. And two, he wanted me to write the screenplay. These things really mattered to me. The other studios that had approached me wanted to make Alex older or to release the movie as a "U" certificate. But Marc was talking about a serious action and adventure movie that would appeal to

Anthony with (from left) Marc Samuelson, director Geoffrey Sax and Mickey Rourke

both kids and adults. And if I was writing the screenplay, I'd have the one thing that everyone working on a movie wants – a measure of control. I'd try to make sure that the Alex Rider on the screen was the same Alex Rider I'd created in the books.

■ But why are parts of the movie different to the book?

It may seem strange, after everything I've said, that Anthony Horowitz the screenwriter made so many changes to the work of Anthony Horowitz the writer. But the first thing you have to understand is that as well as my books, I've been writing movies and television for years. I've always known that what appears on the page and what appears on the screen are rarely the same. They're two completely different languages. When I write a book, it's just me – I can do what I like. But when you start work on a movie, two or three hundred people are involved. There's a director who has his own ideas and actors who interpret what's on the page. There's a production designer, director of photography and so on. Look at the credits of any modern movie – they seem to go on longer than the movie itself!

■ Is there anything else you have to consider?

Of course – the budget, the most critical thing of all. Before the money men hand over anything, they want to make sure they're going to make a profit, so they make you work on the script again and again until they're sure you've got it right. In the end, I wrote the script of *Stormbreaker* about fourteen times.

■ Let's look at some of the main things that have changed. For example, why does the book start with a telephone call, yet in the movie, we actually see the death of Ian Rider.

I wanted the movie to open with a bang – I didn't want to start with a funeral, which would have been slow and depressing. It was an excuse to have a really exciting car chase … and one with a difference. This time, the hero doesn't get away. Also, it helps us understand how Alex feels about the death of his uncle if we see the two of them talking together, even if it's only for a moment.

■ What's this with Sabina Pleasure? What's she doing in *Stormbreaker*?

Half the people who go to this movie will be girls and the producers insisted that they'd like to see a girl on the screen. Alex doesn't really meet Sabina until *Skeleton Key*, the third book in the series, but it didn't seem to matter too much to bring her in a little earlier. I was careful to keep the romantic side down to a bare minimum, and in the end I quite liked the way she suddenly appears in the final reel.

I wrote the script of *Stormbreaker* about fourteen times.

9

■ Why have some of the character names changed?

Before a movie is made, there has to be a name search to avoid problems later on, legal or otherwise. Believe it or not, MI6 asked us not to use the name Crawley, so in the movie the character is called Crawford. Does this mean there really is a spy called Crawley? Who knows! Herod Sayle's name changed because of the casting of Mickey Rourke. He just didn't look like a Herod to me so I changed the name to Darrius (and also made him American). As for Jeff Stryker, it turns out that this is the name of a well-known porn star and so it had to be changed! I can't imagine how the name got into the book of *Stormbreaker*! Honestly, it's not what you think!

■ In the book, Alex escapes from the car crusher in a very different way. Why did you change that?

The car crusher escape took me hours to work out. In the book it was fine as I was able to describe every single detail of what was happening, right down to what Alex was thinking. But in the movie, if he just managed to wriggle his way out of the crusher, would it be dramatic enough? I thought not. So then I thought about spy movies and ejector seats and came up with a new idea.

MI6 asked us not to use the name Crawley.

■ Where did the photo booth at the station come from?

This is another big change and I did this mainly because the movie could only be 100 minutes long and I felt we had to get Alex into MI6 as quickly as possible. I thought this would be fun and fast.

■ Why is there a whole new special forces training sequence that isn't in the book?

Actually, the section where K Unit gets captured and Alex helps them escape did appear in my original book version of *Stormbreaker*, but it was cut by the publishers because they felt that the training went on too long. I put it back into the movie because I'd always liked it.

■ Stephen Fry doesn't look much like Smithers. Did that matter to you?

Stephen is a very well-known actor. It's true that he's not fat, nor is he bald with several chins, although perhaps one day... There are a few actors in the movie who don't look exactly how I imagined them. Look at Mickey Rourke as Sayle or Sophie Okonedo as Mrs Jones. But when actors as good as these say yes to a part in your movie, you don't worry if their appearance is slightly different. A movie isn't an exact copy of a book, and the important thing is not to think about what you may have lost, but how much in freshness and star appeal you will have gained.

■ Why the new gadget – the fountain pen?

At the end of the book, Alex has to make Mr Grin fly him to London. In the book, he brings out a gun. But we couldn't do that in the movie because there are rules that say you're not allowed to. I spent ages wrestling with the problem: if Alex wasn't allowed to threaten Mr Grin, how could he make him do what he wanted? The pen was the answer.

■ Why do Nadia Vole and Jack Starbright have a fight?

Perhaps this is the right time to own up and admit

that not all the ideas in the script were my own. I was getting notes all the time. There was a script editor and I had dozens of meetings with Marc Samuelson and the director, Geoffrey Sax, who added a lot of jokes of his own. So, as the movie had two great actresses, Alicia Silverstone and Missi Pyle, someone thought it would be a good idea to throw them together. I agreed.

■ What happened to the submarine? And why use a helicopter and not a cargo plane?

The producers couldn't afford the sub. Not after the quad bikes, the Jeeps, the Hummers and all the rest of it. They couldn't afford a cargo plane either. Be fair. $40 million will only go so far!

Forty million dollars will only go so far!

■ What happened to the chase in the cornfield?

The quad bike chase was in the original script but we all felt that enough was enough. Believe it or not, it is possible to have too much action in an action movie, and anyway, there was going to be a quad bike chase later on when Alex escapes from Sayle Enterprises. I also cut the scene in the library and shortened the journey through the mine. Everyone felt that as we moved into the last third of the movie, we had to get to the Science Museum as quickly as possible.

■ Where did the horseback chase come from?

To be honest, I wasn't exactly crazy about Alex and Sabina galloping on a horse across London. But the producer and the director loved it and in the end I lost the argument. We had to get Alex from the Science Museum in West London to

Sayle's office in the City (a distance of about four miles) and I couldn't think of a better alternative. It also gives Sabina a proper role and allows her to get drawn into the climax. And watching the camera trucks roaring up and down Rotten Row, chasing the Household Guards who were chasing Alex and Sabina, I had to admit I was probably wrong.

■ Wait a minute – the whole end of the movie is different! What's that all about?

When I first wrote the screenplay, I finished it exactly the same way as the book. Sayle kidnaps Alex and takes him to a heliport on the top of a skyscraper. But everyone felt that after all the excitement in the Science Museum, the last section of the movie was a bit of a let-down. That's one of the rules about a modern action and adventure movie – it has to get bigger and bigger until it stops. The kidnap sequence was just a bit small. So we talked about it and we came up with the idea of a back-up transmitter, which would allow us to have one last fight high above London – a great way to finish a great movie!

The Alex Rider books...

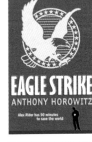
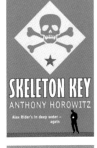

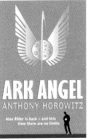

The Movers and Shakers

PRODUCERS:

Stormbreaker is produced by Marc and Peter Samuelson, (*Arlington Road, Wilde, Revenge of the Nerds* and *Tom & Viv*), Steve Christian (*Revolver, The Libertine*) and Andreas Grosch (*All the King's Men, The Jacket*). Hilary Dugdale, Nigel Green, Anthony Horowitz and Andreas Schmid are executive producers. The line producer is Kevan Van Thompson, with Jessica Parker as associate producer.

DIRECTOR:

Geoffrey Sax has had a long and varied career in movie and television, and his recent feature film *White Noise*, starring Michael Keaton, was an instant success on both sides of the Atlantic in 2005. His television credits include *Tipping the Velvet, Othello, Clocking Off* and *Rowan Atkinson Presents*.

DIRECTOR OF PHOTOGRAPHY:

BAFTA®-award-winner Chris Seager began his career in 1984, as a camera operator on the television series *Just Good Friends*. Since then he has worked as a cinematographer on more than 30 television series, including the multi-award-winning *Yes, Prime Minister*. His first feature film was *White Noise*.

SCREENWRITER:

Anthony Horowitz is a successful novelist and screenwriter. His television credits include the television series *Poirot, Midsomer Murders* and *Foyle's War*. He's one of the few children's book authors who is a household name. *Stormbreaker*, the first in Anthony's bestselling Alex Rider series, was named in a nationwide poll of children as the book they most wanted to see turned into a movie.

PRODUCTION DESIGNER:

Ricky Eyres was nominated for an Emmy® for his art direction on *The Young Indiana Jones Chronicles*. His other past television credits include *Farscape* and *Farscape: The Peacekeeper Wars*. Ricky's movie credits as art director include *Alfie, The Parole Officer, The Beach, The Lost Son, Star Wars Episode I: The Phantom Menace, Saving Private Ryan, The Jackal, Edward II* and *Nightbreed*.

EDITOR:

Andrew MacRitchie recently edited the feature films *Die Another Day* and *Sahara*. He began his career as an assistant editor working on movies such as *Spies Like Us, The Princess Bride, Willow, Who Framed Roger Rabbit*, and *Indiana Jones and the Last Crusade*. As first assistant editor he worked on the Oscar®- and BAFTA®-award-winning movie *Elizabeth*.

STUNT COORDINATOR:

Lee Sheward started out as a circus aerialist, before changing careers to work as a stunt performer and coordinator. He has worked on more than 100 television programmes and movies, including *Batman*, *Interview with the Vampire*, *Mission: Impossible*, *The English Patient*, *Titanic*, *The World Is Not Enough*, *Billy Elliot*, *The Pianist*, *Love Actually*, *The Bourne Supremacy*, *The Hitchhiker's Guide to the Galaxy* and *The Gathering*.

COSTUME DESIGNER:

John Bloomfield won a BAFTA® for his work on the award-winning television series *The Six Wives of Henry VIII*. Since then he has worked as costume designer on the feature films *Conan the Barbarian*, *Robin Hood: Prince of Thieves* (for which he received a BAFTA® nomination), *The Mummy*, *The Mummy Returns*, *The Scorpion King*, *Open Range* and *Being Julia*.

HAIR AND MAKE-UP DESIGNER:

Kirstin Chalmers has worked on a variety of television and movie productions, including Guy Ritchie's *Revolver*, *Around the World in 80 Days*, *Piccadilly Jim*, and Mike Leigh's *All or Nothing* and *Topsy-Turvy*. Her work on Laurence Dunmore's commercial *Would I?* won the BTCA Award for Best Make-Up and Prosthetics.

CALLING THE SHOTS
THE DIRECTOR

Geoffrey Sax had always wanted to make a British movie that would compete with the best of Hollywood, as well as one that his children could watch. So when the chance came to direct *Stormbreaker*, he did not hesitate. "I wanted to make a thoroughly entertaining movie that didn't patronise or preach to its audience," he says. "The key thing that I wanted the whole cast and crew to understand was that they should try to forget that it was a movie about a teenager. We treated it as an adult movie with the production standards you'd expect in an adult action movie."

When Sayle captures Alex, for example, it was important to Sax that the audience felt he was in real danger. "You have to believe they are willing to kill him," he says. Although larger-than-life characters such as Nadia Vole and Mr Grin do add comedy to the movie, Sax was careful never to let the actors go too far. "The temptation is to go over the top, but if you do that you lose the tension and the suspense," he explains.

Sax lived and breathed *Stormbreaker* for the whole of its twelve-month production schedule. He was involved at every stage, from the initial planning and main shoot, to the editing and post-production process. "I didn't have a single day off the entire time we were shooting!" he says. "You have to pace yourself, and prepare thoroughly. But it was definitely worth it and I'd do it again for sure!"

Meet Alex Rider

In 2000, Walker Books published *Stormbreaker*, which introduced Alex Rider to the world. Determined to investigate his uncle's death in a mysterious car accident, Alex discovers that the man who had brought him up was not a banker, as he claimed, but a secret agent, and Alex is forced to take his place.

Alex Rider is a boy who just wants to lead an ordinary life. He is devastated by his uncle's untimely death, but even more unsettled when he learns that his own special skills – his black belt in karate, his knowledge of foreign languages, and his extreme sports training – were all just part of a plan to prepare him for a career in MI6. "Alex is the reluctant spy," says Anthony Horowitz. "He's not having a good time. In every book he's manipulated, lied to, twisted into getting involved in these adventures."

The books immediately struck a chord with a huge audience of children – and adults too! Since the publication of *Stormbreaker*, Alex Rider's six adventures have sold nine million copies worldwide and been translated into twenty-eight languages. Their runaway success shows no sign of slowing down – despite the shocking cliffhanger ending of the fifth book, *Scorpia*. "Alex took a sniper's bullet and was left lying, seemingly dead, on the pavement," Anthony says. "Although I was never going to get rid of him I did think I'd have a little rest. But there were so many letters to the publisher, e-mails to me, and general upset and dismay, that I decided I had to bring him back fairly fast, in *Ark Angel*. I don't think I will ever kill Alex – I like him too much to ever want to hurt him."

Anthony believes that much of Alex's distinctive appeal comes from the dangerous adult world that he is thrown into. He says, "The Alex Rider world is meant to be cold, hard and serious, although hopefully fun and exciting at the same time."

ALEX PETTYFER

Early in 2005, the search began for the young actor who would be Alex Rider. Fans from all over the world began campaigning for their favourite actors or their friends and in many cases themselves too to be cast as their hero.

Co-ordinated by casting director Sarah Bird, the process involved auditioning more than 500 teenagers. As Marc Samuelson explains: "It's much more efficient for the casting director to visit a school, sift through a hundred boys and then bring in just eight or ten of them to an audition than it would be opening hundreds of letters and e-mails from people who write in – because, sadly, 99.9% are completely unsuitable and you know within seconds." Marc adds, "It's very interesting the way you have some fabulous looking boys who can't really act and then you have some fabulous actors who don't have the looks. Fortunately, Alex Pettyfer has it all so we were very happy to cast him. He has fantastic looks and is great in the action scenes. He runs very well, he can fight, he is physically strong and he's done quite a lot of training. It really shows because he has to fight people who are much bigger than him, and it's totally credible."

"When they said 'We'd like you to play Alex Rider' I was blown away, really excited," explains Pettyfer. "I'd already been to about five auditions and when I was called back I thought it was another audition, but I couldn't see anybody else, and that's when they said I had the part. There are a lot of people out there who wanted this opportunity and it's been given to me and, hopefully, I'll be doing it for all those guys who didn't get it."

Pettyfer adds, "Who wouldn't want to play Alex Rider? It's the best character for a teenager to play. Anthony wanted to show the reality of being a spy. It's not a perfect world – it's a lonely and daunting experience for a kid of fourteen."

Alex Pettyfer

Born: Windsor, Berkshire, UK
Date of birth: 10 April 1990

- took the leading role in the popular television drama, *Tom Brown's Schooldays*
- first appeared on television in a yogurt commercial, aged six
- Alex's hobbies include skiing and hockey

"He's great – really handsome and he's got the movie star thing down really well."
ALICIA SILVERSTONE

It all begins... At Slater's Auto Wrecking

Alex and Jack Starbright are returning from the funeral of Ian Rider when they spot two men carrying boxes out of their house – boxes full of Ian's personal belongings. Alex gives chase on his bike and follows them to Slater's Auto Wrecking, where he makes a terrifying discovery: Ian Rider did not die in a car crash. His BMW is riddled with bullet holes!

Alex is forced to hide in his uncle's car to avoid discovery, but is almost killed when it is dropped into the car crusher. As the iron jaws close in, Alex discovers a secret ejector seat mechanism, and is shot to safety with only seconds to spare! However, his relief is short-lived as he is set upon by the wrecking crew. Alex's black-belt karate skills come in handy as he fights them off and makes his escape.

Kung Fu legend Donnie Yen designed the fight scene at Slater's Auto Wrecking. He says, "It was rewarding to work with Alex Pettyfer. This was his first time making a Hong Kong-style action scene, and he came through good!" Alex agrees. "Donnie is great to work with – I think that when you click with someone and like working through the day with them it's so much easier."

Alex, who had no martial arts experience before working on *Stormbreaker*, trained with his stunt double Eunice Huthart, a European champion kick-boxer. Alex says, "I went in there fresh with Eunice. We started off with the basics, just seeing how I could kick or punch, and it went on from there to Jiu-jitsu and street-fighting."

Alex on Alex

So how did Alex Pettyfer feel when he got the lead role in the biggest British children's movie ever – and what was it like working with *Stormbreaker*'s star-studded cast? Alex reveals all, in his own words.

When I first met Anthony Horowitz, the only thing I wanted from him was information, anything that could help me build the character. But we ended up good friends.

I don't really talk to my friends about what goes on during filming because I just want to feel that I'm the same as them – I don't want to talk about movies or action. I just want to go back to school and have fun with them.

After they told me I'd got the part in Stormbreaker, I went home and sat down and it was as if the walls were closing in on me. I'd either made the worst decision in my career or the best – at the time I didn't know.

We spent three to four hours a day fighting, but I was never tired. I was enjoying myself. It was great.

Alicia is fantastic as Jack. She's a great actress. She started her career the same age as me and worked her way up. I hope to follow in her footsteps.

Donnie Yen is one of the best martial arts fighters in the world. He came with a team of four stuntmen and they were fantastic – so agile, fit and fast. But the main thing he taught me was peace and tranquility.

Jumping Jack

Alicia Silverstone

Born: San Francisco, California, USA
Date of birth: 4 October 1976

- her parents are English
- starred in *Clueless*, *Blast from the Past*, *Love's Labours Lost* and *Batman and Robin*
- is a vegan and has strong views on animal welfare

"Alicia was in our thoughts from the very beginning, because Jack is the all-American girl. The girl next door, your big sister, your best friend – that's Alicia. She's a great actress, a delightful team player and somebody everyone loved having around."
MARC SAMUELSON

"Alicia's delightful, incredibly professional and inventive. She has a genuine sense of comic timing, which is something you can't direct – you either have it or you don't. She's absolutely as I imagined Jack to be from reading the book. "
GEOFFREY SAX

Jack Starbright came to England as a student from America and accepted the job as Ian Rider's housekeeper. It is Jack who looks after Alex following his uncle's death. Alicia Silverstone, who plays Jack, says, "Jack's had the job for nine years, since Alex was little, and she's become really attached – I don't think she could leave. She's like his big sister and best friend."

The first time we see Jack she is wearing a kimono and a Japanese headband and is preparing a sushi dinner that includes a poisonous fugu fish. "Maybe the week before she was belly-dancing around the room and having some kind of Moroccan meal," says Alicia. "She gets into character, it makes it fun for her – I think she thinks she's entertaining Alex, but mostly she's just entertaining herself. She's like a big kid!"

It wasn't all fun and games, however. Later in the movie, Jack has to fight for her life against the villainous Nadia Vole. "We did all these amazing, intense stunts," said Alicia. "We only had one or two rehearsals, so you just threw yourself into it as much as you could and hoped that it'd be great! You do get bruised a lot doing fight scenes, but your adrenalin's going – you're so excited you don't even notice what's happening!"

Alicia had a great time working on *Stormbreaker*. "It's just been an amazing job and it didn't feel like work – especially when I was working with Bill Nighy and Sophie Okonedo. I'm totally in love with them both and had so much fun. I feel very lucky to be part of such an amazing cast."

Everybody was Kung Fu Fighting

Stormbreaker's amazing martial arts sequences are the work of Hong Kong movie legend Donnie Yen. Donnie brought more than twenty years of experience as an actor, stunt performer and director to the shoot – as well as some unfamiliar ways of working.

Donnie explains, "In Asia, the Martial Arts Choreographer not only choreographs the scenes but he actually directs them too. However, in Western cinema they usually hire a choreographer just to work out the movements, leaving the director to figure out how to shoot the fight. This can mean they end up shooting the whole fight from five different angles, having to then put it all together in the editing room. But when you watch Hong Kong movies the action looks the way it was envisaged to begin with – the choreographer edits the action in their head before the shoot."

Producer Marc Samuelson agrees. "The fights are brilliantly put together. I think the crew felt this was an amazing way of doing it and they've picked up some interesting tips along the way."

Spectacular as the fight scenes are, Donnie explains that it's important they blend in with the style of the movie, "It's not about choreographing a bunch of acrobatic movements. It's about playing the character, so I try to put myself in that position – how would Jack Starbright react when Nadia Vole tries to hit her? If you concentrate on the characters, all the movements come naturally."

Donnie was particularly pleased with Alex's fight at Slater's Auto Wrecking. Donnie created a "rope dart" sequence for Alex in which he attacks Slater's wrecking crew using a heavy length of rope – an ancient martial arts technique, which requires extraordinary hand-eye co-ordination. Even though Alex had had no training, Donnie regards the sequence as one of the best he has choreographed.

Bad Boy Bikes and Kick-Ass Cars

Yamaha WR450F

- liquid-cooled, 4-stroke, 449cc, 5-valve, DOHC engine
- wide-ratio 5-speed transmission
- multi-plate wet clutch
- digital CDI ignition

Yamaha manufacture the WR450F in blue only so all the bikes used in the movie had to be re-sprayed in black and in red. To improve bike performance both the exhausts and tyres were replaced. The new tyres allowed the drivers to accelerate super-fast, brake suddenly, and hug corners – all essential features given the demands of the stunts. One of the bikes was further adapted to carry a camera for the point of view shots, giving us a unique view from the driver's perspective.

This off-road motorcycle is the mount of choice for Sayle's security teams – fast, manoeuvrable, and now available in two custom colours: Bad Boy Black or Rider Red.

With four-wheel drive and rugged styling, this All-Terrain Vehicle won't let a superhero down in a tight spot.

Yamaha Grizzly 660

- single cylinder, 4-stroke, liquid-cooled, 660cc, 5-valve engine
- On-Command™ 2WD/4WD differential lock
- all-wheel hydraulic disc brakes
- independent double wishbone suspension

For safety reasons, Alex Pettyfer's quad bike had the throttle restricted to reduce the machine's speed. The quad used by Alex's stunt double was stripped down and rigged for the runway crash scene: all heavy and flammable elements were removed and special effects added, including pyrotechnics and explosives. To accommodate Alex's harpoon, the rear luggage rack on his quad was raised allowing the weapon to slide in easily.

BMW Z4 Roadster
- capable of 140 mph
- 2.5 litre 6-cylinder, 4-valve engine
- 5-speed manual transmission
- independent front and rear suspension
- sequential electronic fuel injection system

Four roadsters were used in the movie; two were stripped down and modified for the interior shots of the car crusher scene and two were used for shooting at a distance, such as the drive-bys.

Perfect for those road rage moments, Smithers has installed rear-mounted guided missiles in Agent Rider's car.

Hummer H2
- 6.0 litre V8 engine
- 4-speed electronically-controlled automatic transmission
- variable-ratio power steering
- 4-wheel disc braking with ABS

Just two Hummers were used for all interior and exterior shots in the movie. And, like all other Sayle industry vehicles, the black Hummers had their number plates removed making them look more unusual and mysterious.

Highly recommended by PR consultant Nadia Vole for all your secret mission needs. It's strong enough for a man, and powerful enough for a crazed henchwoman.

Fletcher Sportcruiser powerboat
- power-assisted steering
- 215 horsepower engine
- 101.25l fuel tank
- comes with sink and cooker

The Fletcher powerboat was re-sprayed from white to black and fitted with a performance propeller to make the boat go faster.

Ideal for coastal patrols, its cabin is roomy enough for six hired killers and their bazookas.

Story so far... LIVERPOOL STREET STATION

Alex escaped from Slater's Auto Wrecking with just one clue – Slater was taking Ian Rider's belongings to Liverpool Street Station. Armed with this vital piece of information, Alex races off to the station in the hope of intercepting him. But instead, Alex and Jack spot Crawford, one of Ian Rider's bank colleagues, and decide to follow him.

Crawford goes into an automatic photo booth, but a moment later someone completely different comes out! When Alex goes in, he is whisked away down a hidden tunnel to emerge in the secret underground headquarters of MI6's Special Operations Department.

He is met by Alan Blunt, the Head of Special Operations, and his deputy, Mrs Jones. They reveal to Alex that his uncle was a spy, and that they want him to take Ian's place investigating Sayle Enterprises in Cornwall – the assignment that got him killed. Alex refuses, but Blunt makes it clear that Jack's visa will be revoked if he doesn't agree, so Alex is left with no choice.

The comedian Jimmy Carr plays the small but vital role of Crawford. Marc Samuelson says, "Every casting decision on the movie had a lot of thought put into it. In Jimmy's case, we wanted someone who had an odd, unsettling manner, and he fit the bill perfectly." Jimmy jokes, "I like to think I will get a spin-off movie based on Crawford – he'll be office-based, probably doing internet research and the odd bit of translating. It won't be as exciting as *Stormbreaker*, but a lot cheaper to shoot!"

MI6 – Special Operations

The real MI6, officially known as the Secret Intelligence Service, was founded in 1909. It was set up to oversee the United Kingdom's overseas espionage missions. In World Wars I and II, MI6 ran networks of secret agents in occupied Europe. During the Cold War, MI6 was heavily involved in spying on the Soviet Union. In the 1950s, great damage was caused by Soviet spies infiltrating MI6 itself, such as the infamous "Cambridge Spy Ring" led by Kim Philby. One of the Cambridge spies was Anthony Blunt, who lends his name to a character in *Stormbreaker*. Since then, MI6 has moved to ultra-modern offices in Vauxhall Cross. In the movie, however, MI6 Special Operations is based in secret headquarters accessed from Liverpool Street Station.

Alan Blunt, played by Bill Nighy, is the head of MI6 in *Stormbreaker*. A cold-hearted bureaucrat, he has no scruples about sending Alex into mortal danger – even when the same assignment got Ian Rider killed. Bill Nighy says, "Alan Blunt is a very satisfying character to play. He's spooky but comic: the grey man in the grey suit with the grey hair and the grey glasses. He appears to have no feelings whatsoever. Mrs Jones is the one who does the feeling, Blunt just does the strategy, although when Alex does well, the ice around Blunt's heart melts."

Mrs Jones, played by Sophie Okonedo, is head of the Special Operations department of MI6, reporting directly to Alan Blunt. She is cool, calm and professional, but cannot help wondering whether recruiting Alex Rider is a good idea. "She's tough but compassionate and motherly," says Marc Samuelson. "If Jack is Alex's big sister, Mrs Jones is his mother."

Bill Nighy

Name: William Francis Nighy
Born: Caterham, Surrey, UK
Date of birth: 12 December 1949

- starred in *Love Actually, Underworld, Shaun of the Dead* and *The Constant Gardener*

"I worked with Bill Nighy about 15 years ago on a TV show. He hasn't changed one bit – he's still the director's dream. If I was filming the London telephone directory, I would cast Bill to read it, because he would make it interesting! I think he's the best actor in Britain."
GEOFFREY SAX

Sophie Okonedo

Born: London, UK
Date of birth: 1 January 1969

- starred in *Dirty Pretty Things, Aeon Flux* and *Hotel Rwanda* for which she was Oscar®-nominated

"She's fabulous and brings real class to the movie."
GEOFFREY SAX

Gadgets, Gizmos and Smithers

Where would a movie superspy be without his gadgets? Luckily for Alex, he has his very own gadget master, Smithers, to kit him out with the latest top-secret devices. Smithers is Head of the Covert Weapons Division of MI6. After years of designing secret weapons for MI6 spies, this new assignment comes as light relief. He enjoys the challenge of inventing gadgets that can be carried by a fourteen-year-old boy without arousing suspicion – and ultimately they save Alex's life on more than one occasion.

Stephen Fry, who plays Smithers, says, "I have thirteen godchildren, of whom at least half are absolutely passionate about the Alex Rider books. Smithers, though, is not very fond of children. For this assignment, he has a back room in Hamley's toy shop where he manufactures and lashes together all his clever gadgets. And I imagine he was once a field officer, so I've given him a limp."

Backpack
Alex's smart new backpack is the perfect thing to take on a plane – it's compact and contains a lightweight nylon parachute for those moments when you absolutely have to make a quick exit!

Nintendo DS
It's the latest must-have hand-held games console – although this one comes with a few hidden extras. With the correct cartridge inserted it can turn into a bug detector, a surveillance microphone, or even a smoke bomb. All this and it plays games too!

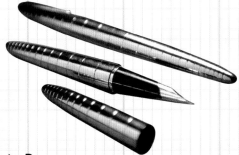

Fountain Pen

The pen is mightier than the sword, at least when MI6 is involved! A compressed gas canister built into the barrel of this elegant fountain pen can shoot the nib six metres. It is loaded with sodium pentothal, which means the unlucky target can be told exactly what to do while under the influence of the drug.

Yo-yo

This sleek metallic yo-yo conceals a powerful motor and winch system capable of lifting up to 90 lbs. With a heavy-duty electromagnet built in, it can be securely clamped to metallic surfaces. The yo-yo cord is a specially-developed super nylon that is virtually unbreakable.

Zit Cream

This ordinary-looking tube of spot cream has a secret ingredient – a special acid that is harmless on skin, but powerful enough to burn through solid steel like a hot knife through butter.

Stephen Fry

Name: Stephen John Fry
Born: London, UK
Date of birth: 24 August 1957

- starred in *Blackadder, Jeeves and Wooster, Wilde, Gosford Park,* and *Tom Brown's Schooldays*
- first met Alex Pettyfer on the set of *Tom Brown's Schooldays*
- is a successful novelist, television presenter, playwright and movie director

"Stephen is such a thorough actor and just turning up and reading lines is not for him. He created a whole character history for Smithers."
MARC SAMUELSON

Story so far... SURVIVING THE SPECIAL FORCES

As part of the preparation for his undercover mission, Alex is sent on a crash course in survival with a trainee special forces unit in the Brecon Beacons. At first, his team-mates resent him being there, but when they are faced with disaster, Alex saves the day.

Alex and "K" Unit are put through a series of gruelling exercises, including assault courses, cross-country runs and a perilous rope-slide. The final test sends the new recruits on a night-time training mission "behind enemy lines", but a mistake by Wolf, their leader, gets them captured by the opposition: a unit of regular army soldiers only too happy to see their rivals humiliated. Locked up in an abandoned farmhouse, "K" Unit is facing the end of their hopes of joining the elite special forces.

Code names
Wolf is the code name of the leader of "K" unit – the special forces team that Alex is attached to on his training course. The other members of the team are Bear, Eagle and Fox. Alex is called Cub.

Alex discovers a bricked-up chimney and breaks it open with a karate kick; the chimney is only just wide enough for him to climb. He makes his way outside, successfully evading the guards, and manages to get to the soldiers' GRASS shelter. He removes the brakes, sending the shelter hurtling down the hillside and off a one hundred foot drop into the freezing waters of the lake below.

The special forces scenes were shot on the Isle of Man, where the art department, under Production Designer Ricky Eyres, built an entire assault course. Ashley Walters, who plays Wolf, says, "It was full on out there every day. One night they had us crawling through mud and water at two in the morning! Constantly freezing, soaked to the skin! It was hard sometimes, but at the same time enjoyable – you got to be a kid again."

How did they do that? THE GRASS SHELTER

The runaway GRASS shelter was, in effect, a huge remote-control car. Chris Seager, the Director of Photography, remembers that "it was quite difficult to direct the shelter using remote control, as the ground was uneven and kept throwing us off course! We had to do a few takes before we got it right."

In the finished movie, the shelter had to appear to fly up over the lip of a cliff and into a lake – but there was no cliff or lake at the farmhouse location. In order to create the effect, the crew first drove the shelter down a long hillside that had a small upward slope at the end. Then they went to a quarry elsewhere on the Isle of Man and filmed the GRASS shelter being driven up and over the edge of a cliff. In post-production the two locations were put together using a computer in a process called compositing, so that it looked as if the upward slope at the end of the hillside was actually the lip of the cliff. Finally, a team of computer graphics artists added in a detailed picture of a lake at the foot of the cliff, complete with ripples in the water.

The actors playing the soldiers wisely removed themselves from the shelter before it was driven down the hillside – not to mention into the quarry!

Alex on Alex

While Alex Rider was being drawn deeper into the world of international espionage, Alex Pettyfer got to know his co-stars – and began to get to grips with his own character.

Bill Nighy and Sophie Okonedo made me laugh all the time. Bill had amazing charisma, Sophie showed me how to keep my energy levels up, and Jimmy Carr just kept cracking jokes.

I felt the turning point in the movie for Alex is when he falls into the water. He comes out changed – it's where it all comes together for him.

I didn't get to spend much time with Stephen Fry but it was good to see a familiar face.

I met a special forces guy during filming. He was very silent, never gave anything away – I like that, and it helped me a lot with the character of Alex.

Sayle of the Century

Darrius Sayle

Darrius Sayle grew up in a trailer park in a tough neighbourhood in South Central Los Angeles. His mother won a million dollars in the California State Lottery, and decided that young Darrius should get away from his dangerous surroundings. He was sent to a top boarding school in the UK, where he found himself in the same class as the boy who would one day become the Prime Minister.

Sayle's time at school was an unhappy one. Bullied because of his underprivileged upbringing, he grew to resent Britain, British schoolchildren, and in particular his prime tormentor, the future PM.

Throughout his meteoric rise to the top of the international computer industry, Sayle never let go of his hatred – a hatred which has become homicidal madness with the creation of the Stormbreaker project.

Sayle Enterprises has agreed to donate one of its revolutionary new computer systems to every school in the country. But unbeknown to the grateful British government, each one contains a deadly surprise: a vial of the genetically-engineered virus, R5. Once the Stormbreakers are activated by radio signal the virus will be unleashed on the unsuspecting schoolchildren. In the final bitter twist to Sayle's long-awaited revenge the signal will be sent out by the Prime Minister himself at the official launch ceremony.

But even Darrius Sayle has not reckoned with Alex Rider...

Mickey Rourke

Name: Phillip "Mickey" Rourke
Born: Schenectady, New York, USA
Date of birth: 16 September 1956

- starred in *Rumble Fish, Diner, A Prayer for the Dying* and *Sin City*
- fought as a professional boxer under the name "El Marielito"
- his Chihuahua "Loki" goes everywhere with him and was on set throughout the shooting of *Stormbreaker*. Mickey had Loki flown over specially from his Los Angeles home.

"Working with Mickey was quite an event-filled experience ... we all have real affection for him. He certainly livened up the set."
MARC SAMUELSON

"He brings undeniable star quality with him and it's interesting being in a room with someone who has that – he has it in bucket loads."
DAMIAN LEWIS

Yassen Gregorovich

Gregorovich is the world's most deadly contract assassin. Born in Russia, he trained with the shadowy criminal organization Scorpia, and began a career of murder and terrorism for hire that saw him working for Iraq, Serbia and Libya among many others.

He speaks nine languages fluently and is an expert in hand-to-hand combat, urban warfare, demolitions, and the use of firearms. Hired to assist Darrius Sayle with the Stormbreaker project, it is Gregorovich who kills Ian Rider and oversees the delivery of the R5 virus. Can Alex avenge his uncle's death – or will Yassen have another role to play?

Damian Lewis

Born: London, UK
Date of birth:
11 February 1971

- starred in *Band of Brothers*, *The Forsyte Saga*, *Colditz* and *Chromophobia*
- trained at the Guildhall School of Music and Drama and the Royal Shakespeare Company
- was so convincing playing an American in *Band of Brothers* that his co-stars refused to believe he was British

"I enjoy playing villains, but Yassen was difficult to play as he's not a straightforward villain. You might question his ethical stance on killing people for money, but he isn't completely evil and there is a heart beneath his icy exterior. I think he's cool."
DAMIAN LEWIS

"The brief for casting Yassen was to find someone extremely striking and someone that you would have respect for. Damian has those amazing steely eyes and the presence to carry the role off."
MARC SAMUELSON

Nadia Vole

Nadia Vole is Darrius Sayle's Press and Public Relations Manager ... or pretends to be. In reality, Vole is a ruthless enforcer and security agent for Sayle's organization, trained in martial arts and counter-espionage. She got the better of Ian Rider, but can she survive Jack Starbright's cooking?

Missi Pyle

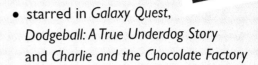

Born: Houston, Texas, USA
Date of birth: 16 November 1972

- starred in *Galaxy Quest*, *Dodgeball: A True Underdog Story* and *Charlie and the Chocolate Factory*

"She has an innate sense of comedy at the same time as being scary and dangerous. Missi is a huge star in the making."
GEOFFREY SAX

Of her role in *Stormbreaker*, Missi says, "It's really fun to do. Playing such a bad character, you have the freedom to be as evil as you wish, which I don't really get enough of in my daily life!"

Andy Serkis

Born: Ruislip, Middlesex, UK
Date of birth: 20 April 1964

- starred as Gollum in the movie versions of the *Lord of the Rings* trilogy
- plays *King Kong* in the remake of the classic monster movie
- is a vegetarian and keen mountaineer

Marc Samuelson was very excited by the casting of Andy Serkis. "Andy is able to use his physicality in very challenging and interesting ways."

"Andy fleshed out Mr Grin into a fully-formed character. I was delighted that we could cast him."
GEOFFREY SAX

Mr Grin

The man known only as Mr Grin once worked in a circus as a knife thrower. The big finish for his act was to catch a spinning knife in his teeth. All went well until his mother came to see the show. A friendly wave from the front row ... a moment of distraction, and the damage was done. The terrible injury that gave Mr Grin his new nickname warped his mind, and he now works as Darrius Sayle's butler and bodyguard – always eager to put his old circus skills to the test.

Story so far... STORMBREAKER

Alex's cover story for his mission is that he's a computer nerd, Kevin Blake, who won a competition in a computer magazine. The prize is a tour of the Sayle Enterprises factory complex, with a chance to try out the new Stormbreaker computer system.

Alex doesn't expect to be impressed by the Stormbreaker – but he can't help but be amazed by Sayle's cutting-edge technology. Strapped into the enormous prototype, Alex is taken on an incredible virtual-reality tour, from the dinosaur-haunted jungles of the Jurassic period to the depths of outer space.

Ricky Eyres says that the design of the Stormbreaker computer system was one of the biggest challenges of the entire movie. "Apart from the Apple Macintosh, most computers look the same – just grey boxes. I had to come up with something new that looked different but was still realistic." Ricky came up with a highly distinctive oval design for the Stormbreaker computer monitor, and this design had a big impact on the look of the rest of the movie. Ricky explains, "All the eye images that you see in the movie – the Sayle Enterprises logo, the advert for the computer with Darrius Sayle looking down on the crowds at Liverpool Street Station – were inspired by the look of the monitor screen."

For the virtual reality sequence, Ricky built a huge prototype Stormbreaker on a giant turntable so that it could revolve 360 degrees. Ricky says, "The rotating bit wasn't in the script, but sometimes you have to find ways to add visual interest to what is on the page." The movie-makers used computer graphics and a special lighting effect to show Alex's body being scanned with lasers.

The Sayle Enterprises logo

How did they do that? SPECIAL EFFECTS

Many of *Stormbreaker*'s shots are created with the blue screen technique. This is a way of combining two or more pieces of film into one so that they look real. For example, when the opening chase sequence was shot, Ewan McGregor was not present, but the movie-makers wanted to show him in Ian Rider's car with the Sayle Enterprises guards pursuing him in the background. On the Isle of Man, the *background plate* was filmed, showing the Sayle Enterprises guards on their motorcycles. Later, in Pinewood Studios, Ewan was filmed. Blue screens were placed all around Ian Rider's car, so that from inside they were the only things visible through the car windows. A computer then turned the footage of Ewan into what is called a *travelling matte* by cutting out any blue in the picture. It works like a stencil: when the matte is laid over the background plate, the background only shows through the holes.

When Alex experiences the virtual-reality world of the Stormbreaker computer, he enters into a complete CGI world. Alex was shot on his own against blue screens so that he could be inserted into these detailed 3-D environments – outer space and a prehistoric jungle complete with dinosaur!

Some of the locations in *Stormbreaker* were put together entirely by CGI (Computer Generated Imagery). Working from Ricky Eyre's detailed drawings and models, the CGI team created a 3-D computer model, effectively a skeleton, for each building. Then, a team of artists created the skin – a *matte painting*. This is a detailed, realistic picture that is laid over the surface of the building to make it look real. The matte paintings are often a collage of many different elements. For example, Darrius Sayle's home includes parts of the dome of St Paul's Cathedral, London.

Sometimes the movie-makers used CGI for set extension. As Ricky Eyres explains, "MI6 is designed like a wheel, with a hub in the middle and the office areas in a circle around it. We only built a segment of that wheel, about 1/6 of it. The CGI team was brought in to fill in the other 5/6, so that it appears much bigger in the movie than it did in real life."

It is not only buildings that get the computer graphics treatment. Some of the creatures in the movie, such as the dinosaur, the bat that startles Alex in Dozmary Mine, or the fish that falls victim to Sayle's pet jellyfish, were created purely through CGI. The level of detail is high; the fish needed a fully moving skeleton so that it would move realistically in the water. Its gills even open and close!

Story so far... IN DOZMARY MINE

Alex has begun to suspect that there's more going on at Sayle Enterprises than meets the eye, and his suspicions are confirmed when he sneaks out of his bedroom one night to investigate. He witnesses the delivery of a mysterious cargo and the murder of a guard at the hand of Sayle's hired gun, Yassen Gregorovich.

Meanwhile, Nadia Vole has hacked into Alex's mobile phone and discovered his secret identity. After a bruising confrontation with Jack Starbright at Alex's London home, Vole reports to Sayle who orders the teenage spy's death. But thanks to Smithers' handy Nintendo surveillance gadget, Alex is forewarned. He slips away from the complex and makes his way to the Dozmary Mine.

The mine is a deserted and forgotten entrance into the restricted areas of Sayle's factory, and Alex is forced to claw his way through its claustrophobic underground tunnels. Inside, he discovers the truth about Sayle's plans – but Alex's luck is about to run out...

The set of the mine shaft was specially constructed to allow the crew to film Alex crawling along the tunnels. As Chris Seager explains, "In the narrow part that Alex had to crawl through, the ceiling was very close to the floor, but to one side it opened up wide enough for us to get a camera crew in. It meant that we could track him all the way without having to squeeze in there ourselves."

Fishy Foes

There's more than a little that's fishy about Darrius Sayle's complex in Port Tallon, and one of Alex's most terrifying foes lives in a reinforced aquarium in Sayle's home. When Alex's cover is blown, he is thrown into the tank to take his chances with the killer Portuguese Man o' War.

Meanwhile, the ruthless Nadia Vole is having problems of her own with a nasty wound caused by a poisonous fugu fish – that'll teach her to gatecrash Jack Starbright's sushi dinner!

Alex's dramatic escape from the jellyfish tank was one of the most tensely-awaited scenes in the whole shooting schedule, and the last to be filmed on Ricky Eyres' spectacular living room set. The set was cleared, the cameras locked into place, and then a charge of Semtex plastic explosive was detonated, blowing out the thick glass walls of the tank and swamping the room with 17,000 gallons of water.

The tank had to be very carefully engineered, not only to hold back the pressure of 60 tons of water but also to be safe for the actors and camera operators who needed to work inside it. The half-ton panes of glass had to be lowered into place by crane. "It was nerve-wracking," said Ricky. "If it had gone wrong, it would have taken days to put the set back together again. But it went perfectly."

Name: Spiny Puffer Fish
(Diodon holocanthus)
Born: Central Pacific Ocean

Diodon was thrilled to get the part in *Stormbreaker*. "I always knew my dramatic spiny skin would pay off one day, and when Takifugu was unavailable, my agent gave me a call," the fish revealed. "It was a great honour to work with Alicia and Missi, although I had to spend a long time in make-up every day being varnished for the big fight scene." Diodon says it would like to do more theatre work. "My first love has always been the stage, darling. Glub."

Name: Portuguese Man o' War, (*Physalia physalis*)
Born: South China Sea

Darrius Sayle's hobby is hunting rare animals, and on one of his expeditions in the South China Sea he encountered this fearsome jellyfish. The Portuguese Man o' War can grow tentacles as long as 55 metres – that's longer than six double-decker buses end to end! They use these tentacles to stun and kill their prey.

Portuguese Man o' War venom is dangerous to humans; the sting is intensely painful and can cause allergic reactions. When Alex breaks the Man o' War's tank, Nadia Vole finds this out first-hand!

Ricky Eyres says of the movie jellyfish, "It's not really a puppet, it's an intelligent prop! The real Portuguese Man o' War is ethereal – like it's made from polythene bags. We felt that it wouldn't work on screen, so our jellyfish has a more physical presence to it."

Name: Tiger Puffer (*Takifugu rubripes*)
Born: Northwest Pacific Ocean

Fugu is a large puffer fish, around 70 cm long, and when threatened can inflate itself by pumping water into its stomach until it looks like a spiny football!

It is an aggressive fish, and has been known to bite the fingertips off the chefs trying to prepare it. But its teeth are not the most deadly weapon in its arsenal. Its body contains a poison called tetrodotoxin, which is more than a thousand times more toxic than cyanide – a good reason for hungry fish to steer clear!

However, fugu is considered a delicacy in Japan where it has been eaten for at least 2000 years. Only specially licensed chefs are allowed to prepare fugu dishes. The most poisonous parts, such as the liver, are removed, and then the meat of the fish is sliced thinly and served raw. The tiny amounts of the toxin in the meat cause a tingling feeling in the mouth.

A few people still die every year from eating fugu, and it is the only food that the Emperor of Japan is not allowed to eat. And you thought *Jaws* was scary!

Story so far... THE GREAT ESCAPE

Having escaped from the Portuguese Man o' War's fishy embrace, Alex races to stop Darrius Sayle from activating the Stormbreaker network. Driving a quad bike stolen from Sayle's guards, he chases the helicopter that Mr Grin is piloting.

Using a harpoon taken from Sayle's collection, Alex spears the chopper just as it is taking off and climbs up the rope, dangling perilously hundreds of feet in the air. Safely on board, he uses the dart from the mind-controlling fountain pen given to him by Smithers to make Mr Grin take him to London. But it's not that simple: Sayle has a head start, and to interrupt his murderous plan in time, Alex will have to drop in on the Science Museum ... literally!

Geoffrey Sax explains how the chase sequence was shot: "There's loads of action with all sorts of vehicles chasing Alex up the runway, so we did lots of takes from all sorts of different angles." To prepare for this scene, Alex had quad bike-riding lessons at Pinewood Studios. He became good enough to perform part of the chase himself. For other shots, the quad bike was attached to the back of a camera vehicle to give the movie-makers more control. This was how they were able to show Alex riding the bike on only two wheels.

Of course, some stunts were too dangerous for *Stormbreaker*'s young star to attempt. "When Alex Pettyfer harpoons the helicopter we put him on a wire rig so that we could show him being jerked up into the air," says Geoffrey. "We couldn't show him actually dangling from the helicopter though – we leave that sort of thing to the professionals!"

How did they do that?

THE SCIENCE MUSEUM

Alex's spectacular entrance to the Science Museum was another example of clever movie-making trickery. Alex Pettyfer didn't do the skydiving sequence himself, as it would have been too dangerous. Instead, the movie-makers created this breathtaking sequence by putting together a variety of different shots. These included Alex suspended on wires from a crane, Alex lying on a trolley with a wind machine blowing into his face, and a close-up of the Science Museum roof taken from a helicopter with a powerful zoom lens. "We needed a shot from Alex's point of view as he descended towards the Museum," says Chris Seager. "We got this by mounting a camera on a helicopter and slowly zooming in on the roof. This gives the impression of falling all the way down into the roof, even though we didn't get any closer than 200 feet."

The scene inside the Museum presented its own problems. Geoffrey Sax says, "We had intended to shoot the scene in the main exhibition hall, which has a glass roof. But at the time it was almost empty with few exhibits. We wanted a more exciting location, and our Location Manager, Jane Soans, managed to get us permission to film in the Making of the Modern World gallery, which was very exciting as it hasn't been done before. That room doesn't have a glass roof, so we had to add one in by computer, along with lots of falling debris."

48

Alex on Alex

In the movie, staying at Sayle Enterprises is a terrifying ordeal for Alex Rider. But for Alex Pettyfer, it was the best part of the shoot...

Mickey was so nice to me. It was strange really – when we were acting together I was thinking, "He's the one I'm supposed to hate." But actually he's the guy I like the most.

Missi is the best actress I've worked with. The characters she builds are just breathtaking. The first time I acted with her she came into the room as Nadia Vole and I just burst out laughing.

Being out there on the quad bike was fantastic – it just brought everything to life. Bullets flying off the side of cars, helicopters, all the rest of it. It's hard to describe.

I have so much respect for Andy Serkis. He's such a nice guy.

Follow that Horse! THE CAVALRY CHARGE

At 6.00 a.m. on a Sunday morning in August 2005, the cast and crew of *Stormbreaker* took over one of London's busiest streets, Piccadilly, to film Alex and Sabina's thrilling horseback ride through the centre of London. It was the first time the street had been shut down for a film, as Marc Samuelson explains: "We had the whole stretch between Green Park and Piccadilly Circus closed, which had never been done before. We'd shoot the actors on horseback weaving in and out of moving traffic – 51 vehicles – and then when they got to the end of the line of traffic all the cars and buses would reverse back to their original positions so we could do another take. It was an amazing sight!"

Sarah Bolger took horse-riding lessons to prepare for this demanding scene, which also involved the use of a mechanical horse on a trolley for some of the more tricky shots. But filming in Piccadilly Circus was even more difficult. Geoffrey Sax says, "We couldn't use horses in the Circus itself, because the cobbles are too slippery, so we filmed a man cycling along blowing a whistle! We got the shots of the public's reaction as they turned round to look. Then, we filmed the actual horse-riding at Pinewood Studios, and replaced the man on a bicycle with the horse by a technical process called Rotoscoping. It's so realistic, I defy anyone to be able to tell the difference!"

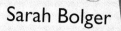

Sarah Bolger

Born: Dublin, Ireland
Date of birth: 28 February 1991

- starred in the acclaimed *In America*, playing the sister of her real-life sister, Emma Bolger
- also appeared in *Tara Road* and *A Love Divided*

"Sabina needed to be feisty, tough and gorgeous, and as soon as our Casting Director suggested Sarah, I knew she was a strong contender for the part."
MARC SAMUELSON

Story so far... SAYLE TOWER

It seems Alex has foiled Sayle's plans, but the villainous billionaire still has one trick up his sleeve. Alex has destroyed the transmitter at the Science Museum, but a backup system remains – built into the roof of Sayle Tower, in the City of London.

Alex and Jack race across London to stop Sayle from activating the Stormbreaker network. In rush-hour traffic, they are getting nowhere fast, until Alex spots his friend Sabina Pleasure taking horse-riding lessons in Hyde Park. Alex and Sabina canter through London's busy streets all the way to Sayle Tower, and are just in time to pull the plug on the transmitter. However, Sayle is not about to let his schemes come to nothing, and a rooftop confrontation leaves Alex and Sabina dangling from a slender cable, 60 storeys above the streets.

The Sayle Tower sequence was filmed at St Mary Axe in the City of London, near the famous "Gherkin" tower. Almost a hundred extras were needed, including 50 dressed as armed police in full counter-terrorism gear. "My wife was on her way to visit the set," remembers Marc Samuelson, "and I got a worried phone call from her saying, 'They've closed off the streets – it looks like some sort of terrorist incident.' I had to explain that it was us!"

The End of the Line...

In the spectacular climax to *Stormbreaker*, both Alex and Sabina are left dangling precariously from a fraying cable, as Jack, Blunt, Mrs Jones and hundreds of horrified onlookers watch helplessly in the streets below. But in his moment of triumph, Sayle is the victim of a stunning betrayal, at the hand of his hired assassin, Yassen Gregorovich.

Sayle had become an embarrassment to Gregorovich's shadowy paymasters, and rather than executing Alex and Sabina, Yassen saves their lives by shooting the crazed billionaire who then topples to his death from the tower's edge. The Stormbreaker project dies with him.

But is Alex's career as a spy also at an end? Only time will tell...

How did they do that? SAYLE TOWER

Sayle Tower itself was shot in the backlot of Pinewood Studios and was one of the movie's largest sets. On all sides were cranes that held huge blue screens, and also black shades, which helped control the sunlight. Using the latest computer technology, the post-production team replaced the areas of blue with other footage. In the case of Sayle Tower, this meant that the set could be made to look bigger, and the London skyline could be filled in, creating a dramatic backdrop.

Shooting the footage was a complex process, and, as Chris Seager explains, occasionally dangerous. "We wanted a shot looking down through the rotor blades of Yassen's helicopter," he says. In order to get this shot Chris, and Marc Wolff the helicopter pilot, had to take part in a daring exercise using a cherry picker, a small vehicle that has an extendable arm, known as a boom, with a platform on the end. Chris explains, "We got hold of a cherry picker, parked it in the middle of a field, got Marc to fly the chopper round and round the cherry picker's boom underneath the platform where we were shooting. I remember thinking, if the chopper clips it, we're all doomed!" Fortunately, Alex Pettyfer and Sarah Bolger were in rather less danger. "They were on wires, with safety harnesses," says Geoffrey Sax, "which are removed – *painted out* – in post-production."

The Stunt Team

Stunt men and women are the unsung heroes of the action movie. They perform hair-raising feats of skill and courage, which require tremendous amounts of thought and planning. They are a small but select group of people, with fewer than 50 registered stunt performers in the UK.

Stormbreaker's stunt sequences were arranged by the highly-experienced stunt coordinator Lee Sheward. One of the most dangerous stunts in *Stormbreaker* was the motorcycle chase sequence. This scene involved five vehicles tearing through the streets and beaches of Port Tallon, and it was almost as perilous for the stunt drivers as it appears in the movie. "I remember thinking, 'I absolutely hate this and I'll be very happy when it's over!'" says Marc Samuelson. "We had two bikes jumping over a boat, and others flying in from the other direction ... it was really dangerous. But all our stunt men were incredibly well-qualified and professional and it went off without a hitch."

Lee Sheward gives out his instructions

The death-defying leap over the sea wall

The stunt team for the motorcycle chase sequence

"The assassination of Ian Rider was quite a technically difficult job," says Lee. "When we rehearsed it, it was a clear summer's day, but on the day we shot it, it was freezing cold and we were fighting the wind – it was very intense!"

The wind was not the only problem. It was very important that Lee did not get too close to Ian Rider's BMW. The exhaust from the helicopter engine, combined with the movement of the rotor blades, created a build-up of static electricity that would have discharged itself into the ground had Lee touched the car – electrocuting him in the process! Lee says, "I brought in Marc Wolff, who's a highly-skilled pilot, to fly the helicopter. He did a great job, so I'm still here!"

Ewan McGregor

Born: Crieff, Perthshire, Scotland
Date of birth: 31 March 1971

- starred in *Shallow Grave*, *Trainspotting*, *Moulin Rouge* and *Star Wars Episodes I–III*

"Ewan is a genuine movie star and he understood instantly what we were trying to do."
MARC SAMUELSON

Costume and Make-Up

Costume designer John Bloomfield's distinguished career in the movies has seen him work mainly on historical drama, but he found that he had no trouble working out his character designs for *Stormbreaker*. "With strong characters like the ones in this movie, you have good ideas about how people should look, even before you know who is playing them," says John. He began drawing before the casting had been finalized, and fine-tuned his designs later to take actors' individual looks into account.

Many of the outfits were made especially for the movie. John contacted clothing manufacturers all over the world to have them create exclusive ranges. He had twenty identical jackets, twenty pairs of jeans and twenty pairs of trainers made up specifically for Alex. It was essential to have twenty of everything, as Stormbreaker's action-packed shooting schedule was tough on Alex's clothes — on some days, as many as six jackets were used.

John particularly enjoyed creating the costume for Missi Pyle's character, Nadia Vole. Missi is 5 foot 11 inches, but John wanted her to look even taller on screen. "I wanted to exaggerate everything about her," he says. "I put her in high heels that made her six inches taller!

Putting the finishing touches to *Stormbreaker*'s cast was Hair and Make-Up Designer, Kirstin Chalmers. Kirstin says, "I read the script several times to become familiar with the story and the characters and then started to build up a picture of what I thought they might look like with sketches, colour charts, and mood boards." Once the actors were cast, Kirstin and her team worked closely with them to develop a look for the character.

"Alex had to look gorgeous without looking too groomed, so he just needed a cool modern haircut and good clean skin," she says.

For grey, humourless Alan Blunt, Kirstin gave Bill Nighy a grey wig, a carefully-trimmed moustache, glasses, a tailored suit, and then used make-up to take the colour out of his face.

"Sophie had short hair that was way too funky for the serious Mrs Jones," explains Kirstin. *So she used a hair piece and a wide head-band with understated make-up to give Mrs Jones a modern take on a 60s look.*

The make-up for the character Mr Grin was the most challenging to create. Kirstin had a specialist make-up effects team sculpt pieces of latex into scar tissue to attach to Andy Serkis's face. Kirstin applied a bald cap, then a thinning wig on top to complete the look. The entire process took two and a half hours.

"Alicia looked pretty near perfect for the role of Jack and so we gave her beautiful natural make-up and tonged her hair to give a tousled girl next door look." As with Alicia, little was needed to change Damian Lewis into the role of Yassen. Mickey Rourke, however, came with facial hair so Kirstin worked around it. She then used a shoulder-length wig, a skin tan and some make-up, creating the flamboyant character of Sayle. Like John, Kirstin found Nadia Vole a rewarding character to work with. "She's such a visual character and Missi has a real physical presence. I gave her dark smoky eyes, red lips and a platinum wig dressed in a 1930's style, creating the look of an evil side-kick!"

The Art of Stage Design

The set designs in *Stormbreaker* were the work of Production Designer Ricky Eyres, who was ultimately responsible for the whole look of the movie. He also had to manage the Art Department, which at times grew to include 120 people. "Working on a movie like this is a marriage of money and art," says Ricky. "You have to co-ordinate all the elements – the set construction, set dressing, props, vehicles and visual effects – and balance the budget, too."

Ricky's preparation for the movie was done on the road. He was constantly sketching in the back of the bus or plane on his way to look at locations. When he had a sketch that he was happy with, it was sent back to the Art Department in London so that work could begin on a model. "I like to model in plaster, because you get a good finish, and you can make it look like stone or concrete. Plus it feels real, which is important to me.

The original drawing of the assembly line set

The assembly line, modelled in plaster

The finished set as it appears in the movie

"When I was designing the sets I was taking inspiration from architecture – trying to get the structure and the geometry of our buildings right. If an environment works structurally then it becomes believable. So my final drawings were all carefully measured architectural drawings, even those buildings that were made up of CGI shots." This was the case with Sayle's house at Port Tallon. Ricky says, "The building was a mixture of classical and modern architectural styles, but tweaked in scale and geometry. I like the idea that the building reflects Sayle's personality. He wants to present himself in a certain way but he gets everything a bit wrong!"

The working drawing of
Sayle's mansion in Port Tallon

Alex on Alex

Alex Pettyfer looks back on an extraordinary feature film debut.

I will be in movies for the rest of my life. If you have a dream you have to follow it, and I've wanted to be an actor since I was eleven.

Everything changes when the cameras start turning. When I'm filming, it's like I'm in a different world. I am Alex Rider. I forget everything else.

I'm going to miss Alex Rider. He was a part of me. Maybe someone else will play him one day but I'll always think it ought to be me.

AFTERWORD BY ANTHONY HOROWITZ

I'm writing this in November 2005 and it's impossible to know at this stage whether the movie will be a success or not. I haven't even seen it yet. Not that it would help much if I had. You can have the best actors in the world, a strong script, terrific production values, and all the rest of it, but what finally completes a movie is you ... the audience. I hope you've enjoyed seeing it as much as we enjoyed making it.

When I began writing the Alex Rider books seven years ago, I never dreamed that I'd one day be at the centre of what is almost an industry. Not just the movie, but the promotions, the socks, the games, the T-shirts, the action figures and all the rest of it. Sometimes I feel hopelessly out of control. But at the same time, I've tried to be true to what made Alex Rider a success in the first place – and it's all been terrific fun.

What next?

Marc Samuelson has asked me to start writing the screenplay for *Point Blanc*. I'm already beginning to worry. Is it right to open the movie with the murder of Michael Roscoe? Will the sequence with Alex hooking the boat on the end of a crane work? I love the ear-stud that's secretly a miniature grenade, but will it look OK on the screen? So many things to think about. And this time Marc didn't even buy me lunch!

First published 2006 by Walker Books Ltd
87 Vauxhall Walk, London SE11 5HJ

2 4 6 8 10 9 7 5 3 1

Text © 2006 Walker Books Ltd
"The Horowitz Interview", "Alex on Alex" and
"Afterword" © 2006 Stormbreaker Productions Ltd
Photographic movie stills © MMVI Samuelsons / IoM Film
Film © MMVI Film & Entertainment VIP Medienfonds 4 GmbH & Co. KG
and UK Film Council

This book has been typeset in Gill Sans
Printed in Italy

British Cataloguing in Publication Data:
a catalogue record for this book is available from the British Library

ISBN-13: 978-1-4063-0339-1
ISBN-10: 1-4063-0339-9

www.walkerbooks.co.uk

Trademarks 2006 Samuelson Productions Ltd
Stormbreaker™, Alex Rider™, Boy with torch logo™, AR logo™

Written by Emil Fortune. Photographer: Liam Daniel

The publisher would like to thank the following
for their kind permission to reproduce their photographs:
Science Photo Library: Georgette Douwma 45 (below centre);
Bauer Millett & Co Ltd: 23 (top right); Yamaha UK: 22 (top right);
Peter Samuelson: 3, 57 (main image)